MW00909470

BUSINESS
SELLING
INSIGHTS

VOL. 6

BUSINESS SELLING INSIGHTS

VOL. 6

SPOTLIGHTS ON LEADING BUSINESS INTERMEDIARIES, BROKERS, AND M&A ADVISORS

FEATURING LEADING BUSINESS INTERMEDIARIES, BROKERS, AND M&A ADVISORS

Sundeep Gill

Robert Cunio

René Brandon

Ron Edmonds

Sheryl Vazquez

Michael Schwantes

Nicholas Brown

Phil Wolfstein

Sheila Spangler

Phil Haney

Copyright © 2022 Remarkable Press™

All rights reserved. No part of this publication may be reproduced, distributed, or transmitted in any form or by any means, including photocopying, recording, or other electronic or mechanical methods, without the prior written, dated, and signed permission of the authors and publisher, except as provided by the United States of America copyright law.

The information presented in this book represents the views of the author as of the date of publication. The author reserves the right to alter and update their opinions based on new conditions. This book is for informational purposes only.

The author and the publisher do not accept any responsibilities for any liabilities resulting from the use of this information. While every attempt has been made to verify the information provided here, the author and the publisher cannot assume any responsibility for errors, inaccuracies, or omissions. Any similarities with people or facts are unintentional.

Business Selling Insights Vol. 6 —1st ed.

Managing Editor/ Shannon Buritz

ISBN: 978-1-954757-24-0

Remarkable Press™

Royalties from the retail sales of **"BUSINESS SELLING INSIGHTS Vol 6: SPOTLIGHTS ON LEADING BUSINESS INTERMEDIARIES, BROKERS, AND M&A ADVISORS"** are donated to the Global Autism Project:

 **AUTISM KNOWS NO BORDERS; FORTUNATELY NEITHER DO WE.®**

The Global Autism Project 501(C)3 is a nonprofit organization that provides training to local individuals in evidence-based practice for individuals with autism.

The Global Autism Project believes that every child has the ability to learn, and their potential should not be limited by geographical bounds.

The Global Autism Project seeks to eliminate the disparity in service provision seen around the world by providing high-quality training to individuals providing services in their local community. This training is made sustainable through regular training trips and contiguous remote training.

You can learn more about the Global Autism Project and make direct donations by visiting **GlobalAutismProject.org.**

CONTENTS

A NOTE TO THE READER

Thank you for obtaining your copy of "BUSINESS SELLING INSIGHTS Vol. 6: Spotlights on Leading Business Intermediaries, Brokers, and M&A Advisors." This book was originally created as a series of live interviews on my business podcast; that's why it reads like a series of conversations, rather than a traditional book that talks at you.

My team and I have personally invited these professionals to share their knowledge because they have demonstrated that they are true advocates for the success of their clients and have shown their great ability to educate the public on the topic of buying and selling businesses.

I wanted you to feel as though the participants and I are talking with you, much like a close friend or relative, and felt that creating the material this way would make it easier for you to grasp the topics and put them to use quickly, rather than wading through hundreds of pages.

So relax, grab a pen and paper, take notes, and get ready to learn some fascinating insights from our Leading Business Intermediaries, Brokers, and M&A Advisors.

Warmest regards,

Mark Imperial
Publisher, Author, and Radio Personality

INTRODUCTION

"BUSINESS SELLING INSIGHTS Vol. 6: Spotlights on Leading Business Intermediaries, Brokers, and M&A Advisors" is a collaborative book series featuring leading professionals from across the country.

Remarkable Press™ would like to extend a heartfelt thank you to all participants who took the time to submit their chapter and offer their support in becoming ambassadors for this project.

100% of the royalties from this book's retail sales will be donated to the Global Autism Project. Should you want to make a direct donation, visit their website at GlobalAutismProject.org

SUNDEEP
GILL

CONVERSATION WITH SUNDEEP GILL

■ **Sundeep, you are the founder of the GillAgency.**
Tell us about your work and the people you help.

Sundeep Gill: We are an M&A advisory firm. We specialize in assisting business owners in lower middle markets, mainly in the technology field, because I have a background in technology. I have a computer science degree from the New York Institute of Technology. But if you were to ask me to code, I don't do any coding whatsoever. I was also recruited to work for Merrill Lynch right out of college. By the time I left my position there, I had run their ERP system. So I'm very well versed in the technology world. In addition, all the businesses I have sold in the past were technology-related, and most of the current engagements I'm representing are also technology-related. I get technology.

■ **How prepared are owners when it comes time to sell their businesses?**

Sundeep Gill: They are not prepared at all. Part of what we do is try to educate business owners. Even if you aren't planning to sell right now, we can do a broker's opinion of valuation or BOV in short and help you create a five-year or a ten-year plan. We don't try to strongarm you into selling right away. If you're not ready today, at least we can guide you so that you can be prepared when you need to be. Sometimes life just happens. So if you already have a BOV, you will know what your company is worth. We can also advise you on maximizing value down the road to get the most bang for your buck when you sell. And the best part is it's all free yet confidential.

■ **What value do you provide business owners? What does your process entail?**

Sundeep Gill: I've been in this business for eight years. And before that, I was actually looking to buy my own business. So I've been on both sides of the spectrum. And when I was in the market to purchase businesses, it was very surprising to see many business brokers who were not engaged at all. So part of the reason why I got into the industry was to change that. We have expertise in knowing our buyers and what they are looking for in terms of types of companies and profit margins. We have an excellent marketing strategy that we employ for each offering. And we don't take on hundreds of thousands of listings; we only take on four or five per year to focus on each one.

At GillAgency, we found our success by being personal and providing our clients with a high standard of care. I need to be focused and know as much about the business as possible so I can intelligently answer questions from the buyers instead of pushing everything over to my client. In addition, we have developed 37 distinct steps in getting businesses successfully sold, from the first conversation to the closing. I know those are a lot of steps, but by the time I'm halfway done with these steps, my clients don't even realize it.

To answer your question, I've had business owners come to me because they couldn't successfully sell their business independently. By the way, I encourage owners to sell their businesses on their own, but it's a daunting task. How do you run a business, which is hard enough as it is, while also trying to find qualified buyers, determine what questions to ask them, and maintain confidentiality? Since I've been doing this for many years, I can guide them through these hurdles and obstacles to get to the closing table. And because I'm an advisor, they can come to me and say, "Hey, Sundeep, I was thinking about giving good bonuses to my key employees because I'm selling the business. What do you think?" and I would say, "No, don't do that, this will decrease your Adjusted EBITDA, and the buyer will find out which in turn will lower the asking price. Instead, give them the same amount or slightly higher to keep them happy." They often rely upon their friends or family for advice who are not subject matter experts. They don't know what the market is doing. So I can help in that area too.

■ **Statistics show that up to 80% of businesses that go to market never sell. What are some reasons for this?**

Sundeep Gill: If I had to pinpoint one thing, I would say lack of follow-ups. When I was in the market to buy a business, very few business brokers followed up with me to say, "Hey, I sent you the confidential information memorandum; what are your thoughts?" I follow up with every buyer who inquires about every offering I have weekly. I'm on top of mind, and it's important because they often come back to me and say, "Oh, I've been meaning to contact you. Thank you for sending that email. How can we move forward?" When you are an M&A Advisor or selling a company by yourself, I believe following up is a crucial part of the process. And that's why a lot of businesses don't sell. Buyers are always looking, similar to real estate. They're almost always looking at something else. So unless you're in front of their faces with a compelling story and a great offering, they're moving on. In addition, getting their questions answered promptly and treating the buyers with respect and care also goes a long way.

■ **Sundeep, what inspired you to get started in this field?**

Sundeep Gill: Growing up, I was always a dealmaker. I'll tell you a funny story. Back in the day, I wanted an Atari game system. One of my friends had one with a couple of games. I was about 11 years old and made a deal with him. I only gave him three games, and he gave me the entire Atari console and five games. The next thing I knew, his mom was over at my house demanding that I return her son's belongings. So it was a good deal for a short while. But that's where it started for me.

Even working for Merrill Lynch, I wanted to be in investment baking. I was bogged down with what I was doing at the time, so I could never get into it. Before I resigned from Merrill Lynch, I bought my own businesses and decided that was how I would retire. So I quit my job after working there for 17 years and got into the nitty-gritty of running those businesses. I didn't like it at all. I was spending 18 to 19 hours a day working. So I ended up divesting and selling the businesses. Then I'm like, "OK, I don't have a job. What will I do next?" The next thing you know, I'm deciding on M&A because I like it. I like the challenge of it. I enjoy helping people and making deals. So I got started working with another company for three years.

Then in the middle of the pandemic in 2020, like many other people, I had a transformation and started GillAgency. I love it. I wake up in the morning looking forward to my calendar, follow-ups, and conference calls. I closed my first deal. We listed it for $7 million and sold it for $8 million. I recently received the IBBA Chairman Council of the Year award under my own banner, GillAgency. I'm very proud of what I do. Again, I love helping people. And even though we are "supposed to be salespeople," I'm not a salesperson. I'm more of a project manager. I'll take on an engagement if I know I can sell it. It hurts me to say I can't sell something, but I don't like giving my clients false narratives. It just wastes everyone's time, and time is more important than money.

■ Is there anything else you would like to share?

Sundeep Gill: Even if you're not considering selling right now, at least get a valuation from a qualified business advisor or M&A advisor. You never know what life may throw at you. Then you will know the value, be aware of any kinks that need to be worked out, and what the industry is doing. Ask your advisor questions like, "What can I do now to sustain growth? How can I maximize profitability when it does come time to sell?" Many people make mistakes along the way. Unfortunately, I must tell some owners, "That ship has sailed for you." And that's a tough thing to tell someone. Creating a plan with a trusted advisor is your best chance at a successful sale.

■ How can people find you, connect with you, and learn more?

Sundeep Gill: My website is gillagency.co. You can also call me directly at 516-218-1590. There's no secretary; there's no gatekeeper. You have direct access to me. You can also email me through the website. We pride ourselves on responding to you within the hour (during business hours).

SUNDEEP GILL

Mergers and Acquisitions Advisor

Founder of GillAgency

Sundeep Gill is based out of New York. Prior to becoming an M&A Advisor, his experience included purchasing and operating four successful businesses. In addition, he was a Vice President at Bank of America/Merrill Lynch, where he spent 17 years overseeing the Research department's ERP system. While there, he managed a large team of individuals and reported to the Chief Operating Officer, where he developed a reputation for successfully completing projects on time.

As a buyer of businesses, he has extensive knowledge of what buyers are looking for and how to negotiate and close a deal successfully. After running his businesses, he decided to divest and successfully sell his companies and focus on the art of deal-making. Having gone through the process of buying and selling businesses, he understands the emotional attachments that owners have to their companies. He considers this while searching for the right potential buyers who will honor the owner's legacy while at the same time negotiating the best terms.

Sundeep has a Bachelor's Degree in Computer Science from the New York Institute of Technology. Sundeep sells businesses worldwide, including the U.S. regions of the Northeast, Midwest, South, and more.

GillAgency

We are a boutique,commission-only business brokerage firm. At GillAgency, we only work with a small number of customers at a time because we only focus on delivering fantastic exits, one business at a time. The high level of commitment required from our end to get such results does not let us take hundreds of listings, like most brokerage firms. As such, we are selective in the companies we work with. Once we get going together, we have no choice but to get a fantastic outcome – we work for free upfront and only get paid if the results are fantastic.

We serve all industries but focus primarily on technology, manufacturing, and distribution. We have five decades of combined experience in buying and selling businesses.

We sell businesses worldwide.

Services Offered

We at GillAgency know you have many options in this crowded field.

So we at GillAgency promise you this:

INTEGRITY - HONESTY - ETHICS - RESPECT

Because we are commission-only, we must stay aggressive to reach the close. By the same token, since we are working towards a common goal as your partner, we are also hyper-focused on getting you the best outcome from the sale – a high premium, a best-fit buyer, and a desired transition and separation for you from your business after the sale.

WE ARE A BOUTIQUE COMMISSION-ONLY BROKERAGE

We are technologists, agile coaches, and lean operation experts, having previously run and sold our technology companies. As such, we build an agile business sale plan and process with you. We do detailed discovery and exit planning at the outset with you. Then we continuously measure the project proceedings against the plan to see if adjustments are needed. As situations arise, we can adjust the plan so that we can always keep our eye on the target – get you the best outcome from the sale of the business – "sell, don't settle" because we are agile, which is why we tackle unforeseen situations efficiently.

EMAIL:

sgill@gillagency.co

PHONE:

516.218.1590

WEBSITE:

gillagency.co

ROBERT
CUNIO

CONVERSATION WITH ROBERT CUNIO

■ **Robert, you are a business advisor with Transworld Business Advisors San Diego Central. Tell us about your work and the people you help.**

Robert Cunio: Simply put, I am in the business of doing good deals for good people. More specifically, I help business owners sell their business, in its current form, to qualified buyers at the best price, or if a business is not quite ready to be sold, I work with the business owner to identify improvements that may be implemented and help them develop a future exit strategy that will ultimately yield the best price sale. Whenever a business owner is ready for a sale, I market the business through various channels, find/vet buyers who would be appropriate to take it over, negotiate the sale, and project manage the escrow process to ensure a successful closing and transition of the business.

■ Do owners know where to start when it comes to selling their businesses?

Robert Cunio: I find that not too many of them do. I would say 95% of the time, the sellers are not experienced with a business sale. For most, growing the business and daily attention to the business operations has been their passion and focus for many years or even decades. For some, it has been a lifetime. A business sale requires a level of expertise that business owners don't necessarily have. Most sellers realize it is best to hire a well-qualified and experienced broker to lead all aspects of the business sale. This allows the seller to continue to run their business and not be distracted by the complicated process and a thicket of issues that can present throughout the business sale, escrow and closing.

■ Are there myths and misconceptions about selling a business?

Robert Cunio: Business owners often think the process should be simple and take much less time than it actually takes. They also believe they can get the highest price by selling on their own. However, sellers come to realize that a broker's expertise is invaluable, and their commission is hard-earned. The commission paid at the close of escrow is well spent as the broker always works in the seller's best interest to maximize a sale price. My personal philosophy is always to do my best to turn tired business owners into retired millionaires.

On average, a good business opportunity takes about nine months to sell and close escrow. A lot of work is involved in the selling process, including the preparation of brochures/consolidation of historical financial data and Confidential Information Memorandums. This must be in place before any advertising/initial marketing and identifying/vetting qualified buyers. Buyers are pre-screened, and those qualified are then bound to Confidentiality Agreements before any business detail is disclosed or confidential data is shared. Then there can be multiple meetings with different buyers to review shared data in greater detail, respond to questions, and present/provide further details on the business. Meetings with multiple buyers can create healthy competition for the business. Maintaining confidentiality with all buyers throughout the process is a critical responsibility of the broker.

Once an offer is received from a buyer, there is a negotiation process, then a due diligence period, escrow project management, and finally, the closing and transition to the new owner. The broker is there for the entire process regardless of how long it may take and is only compensated once the deal is finalized and closed.

■ How far in advance should owners prepare for the sale of their business?

Robert Cunio: This should be a consideration from the get-go. It is essential to start preparing as soon as possible and always keep that possibility first and foremost in mind. Clean and well-organized books and records are critical for the sale of any business, and solid historical data is key to maximization of the ultimate sale price. Minimally, sellers should make this a strict focus three to five years before they are ready to move on. Books and records need to be clean and show stable or, better yet, progressive growth and profitability. If they don't, it may be necessary to make operational and/or financial improvements to the business first, develop a longer-term exit strategy, and then once results are achieved over time, list the business for sale.

■ What value do you provide to business owners?

Robert Cunio: Fundamentally, I take the stress away from business owners so they can focus on running their business and optimizing results. The Bible says in **Matthew 6:34**, "Therefore do not worry about tomorrow, for tomorrow will worry about itself. Each day has enough trouble of its own." I like to think I can be a catalyst for a worry-free business transition.

It is very important for business owners not to become distracted by all of the activities and complexities involved in their business's marketing, sale, and escrow/closing/transition. They should be operating their business and focusing daily on sustaining good results and growth in a way that will attract potential buyers. While they do this, I handle the confidential sale process, so they don't have to worry about any details. This spares business owners the time and aggravation of navigating all of those steps on their own.

■ As we are coming out of a pandemic, is it a good time to buy or sell a business? What are you seeing in your market?

Robert Cunio: Right now is a very good time to sell or buy a business. There was a lot of turbulence and uncertainty during that first year of the pandemic. However, as businesses began to reopen and interest rates remained low, buyer interest in business ownership increased exponentially. Multiple buyers create healthy competition for good businesses, and sellers have been experiencing premium sale prices for their businesses over the past couple of years. The market also remains flush with cash, and lenders have been highly accommodating in financing business sales to qualified buyers. For anyone looking for alternatives with entrepreneurial opportunities, now could not be a better time to explore buying a business.

If you've been following the news over the last few years, you know that business sales are up—*way* up—for certain industries. Record-setting sales (both in terms of speed and profit) in 2021 proved business ownership is in high demand. My advice to sellers is that now is a great time to realize their hard work, make their exit, and leave their business in someone else's capable hands.

■ Robert, what inspired you to get started in this field?

Robert Cunio: I worked in corporate America for over 30 years. I was an executive focusing on Program Management, Contracts, and Finance for a Fortune 500 company. As such, I was often assigned to teams focused on multi-billion dollar mergers, acquisitions, and divestitures and also served as a strategic integrator post-acquisition. So as that company acquired and divested different parts of its business, I was brought in to oversee various elements of that process.

I soon realized I always enjoyed that aspect of my job the most. I decided to pursue that focus as my future career, except on a smaller scale. So I became a business broker and bought a Transworld Franchise in 2016. Now, I do similar work for Main Street America, using my acquired skills over 30 years for mid-range size businesses with $500k to $5M in annual revenue. I absolutely love "doing good deals for good people."

■ Is there anything else you would like to share?

Robert Cunio: Yes, for anyone contemplating selling their business, please register for a complimentary business valuation at my website: https://www.tworld.com/locations/sandiegocentral/sell-a-business/seller-registration/

Understanding your options for business brokerage services in the marketplace is important. Feel free to reach out and ask about Transworld Business Advisors' global network of business brokers and the specific value that working with the leading global enterprise will bring to your business.

■ **How can people find you, connect with you, and learn more?**

Robert Cunio: My website is www.tworld.com/sandiegocentral. Sellers and buyers can find information about my company there and send inquiries to me through the portal. I can also receive emails at rmcunio@tworld.com or rmcunio@gmail.com. Alternatively, please contact me directly at (619) 538-2942. I look forward to connecting.

ROBERT CUNIO, CBI, CBB, MBA

Business Advisor

Transworld Business Advisors San Diego Central

I specialize in turning tired business owners into retired million-aires. I am the Owner/Managing Director of Transworld Business Advisors of San Diego Central and the RMC Realty Group. Through these channels, I have become a trusted Business Advisor and

Realtor to CA Business Owners who engage my services for the sale or acquisition of their businesses and/or commercial properties. I also work with established businesses seeking exponential growth opportunities through franchise development or with sellers pursuing longer-term exit strategies.

As an accomplished and Certified Business Intermediary (CBI), Certified Business Broker (CBB), Master of Business Administration (MBA), and licensed California Realtor (DRE 02005978), I am focused on doing good deals for good people. I always work with an emphasis on enhancing the lives of sellers and buyers and the communities around them.

My background includes over thirty years of working for Fortune 500 companies in the capacity of Business Management and Finance. During this time, I caught the bug for M&A and divestiture initiatives, as I was brought into various multi-billion dollar corporate deals. This was when I caught the bug for what I do now for Main Street businesses. My focus is industry agnostic, although I enjoy certain specialties, including hospitality, manufacturing, marketing, medical, construction/home improvement, entertainment, and health-related businesses.

Whether you desire to sell/buy a business or real property, I offer the professional services necessary to bring buyers and sellers together. My qualification is derived from education and training, extensive business experience, and a passion for achieving optimum results for my clients. I will work smartly and diligently for you and meet or exceed your objectives.

Please see the URL links for more insight into my background and experience, and feel free to contact me directly at rmcunio@tworld. com, rmcunio@gmail.com, or (619) 538-2942 to find out more about my services.

EMAIL:

rmcunio@gmail.com

PHONE:

(619) 538-2942

WEBSITE:

tworld.com/sandiegocentral

FACEBOOK:

https://www.facebook.com/
TransworldBusinessAdvisorsSanDiegoCentral

LINKEDIN:

https://www.linkedin.com/in/robertcunio/

YOUTUBE:

https://www.youtube.com/watch?v=lLMgYJTKMjY&t=36s

RENÉ
BRANDON

RENÉ BRANDON

CONVERSATION WITH RENÉ BRANDON

- **René, you are an M&A Advisor/Broker Associate at Florida Business Exchange. Tell us about your work and the people you help.**

René Brandon: We are business brokers, which means we are licensed the same way as residential real estate brokers in Florida. However, as a business broker, I am licensed to help people buy and sell businesses. We work with Main Street businesses, covering the waterfront - hospitality, manufacturing, distribution, and retail.

- **Do owners know where to start when it comes to selling a business?**

René Brandon: That's an excellent question. As a matter of fact, one of the very first videos I did on my website talks about this very topic. 90% of sellers have never sold a business before, and 90% of all people who buy businesses have never bought a business before.

So it's extremely challenging dealing with those buyers and sellers. They find business brokers primarily through osmosis, meaning they will contact their bank manager, accountant, or lawyer to see if they know anyone, or they go to the internet and do a search. Almost by accident, they fall into the lap of a broker who happens to have a listing they would like to buy or who can give them information about how to sell their business. So it's a very lackadaisical, problematic process that they go through. And frequently, they end up with brokers by default, as opposed to ending up with a broker who may be able to add some value to what they are trying to do.

■ How do you help owners sell their businesses?

René Brandon: Well, let me give you my background because that is how I distinguish myself from all of my peers. I've been in business for over 60 years. I spent 20 years in the corporate world working for Xerox in senior management capacities. Secondly, I've spent 20 years owning and operating my own businesses, including logistics, warehousing, food and beverage distribution, etc. Then for the last 20 years, I've been doing M&A advisory work, as in business brokerage. So given that experience, I understand the process and the journey that a buyer or a seller goes through. I try to cut to the chase very quickly to ensure the approach is realistic and will deliver the results they want.

Buying or selling a business is not like buying a house or selling a house. It's completely different. Buying or selling a house is all about sharing the property, walking through it, and handing out lockbox numbers so potential buyers can have a look. Selling a business is just the opposite. It is highly confidential. Nobody likes to let their employees and competitors know they want to sell their business. Secondly, businesses are very complex animals, and there are lots of moving parts. The whole process of selling a business comprises over 100 different components in terms of looking at the business model, financial statements, staffing, competitors, and marketing. I have experience in all of those areas. So I'm not just going to act as a guardsman or a facilitator in bringing the buyer and the seller together. I go through a lot of trouble analyzing what the seller wants to do and what the buyer wants to do so that we don't waste any time.

■ How are you compensated for your services?

René Brandon: We work on a contingency basis, sometimes called a success fee, a commission based on a portion or percentage of the price paid at closing. It is stipulated in the Seller's Listing Agreement. When the seller is paid, we receive our fee.

■ Statistics show that 80% of businesses that go to market never sell. What are the reasons for this?

René Brandon: Lack of preparation is probably the biggest problem, which means considering all of the factors that a buyer is going to be looking for in terms of buying a business. I try to cover all of those deficits or challenges in selling a business with the seller upfront so that we have a response to any comments that come back from a buyer regarding financial statements, marketing, or staffing. So a big part of my job is preparing the seller appropriately.

But the process is not a "1,2,3" process. If it's done correctly, it can take nine to twelve months between the time we sign an agreement with the seller and when the business is actually sold. Throughout that process, I get to know the business model, strengths and weaknesses, staffing, competition, and other elements mentioned previously. I look at the financial statements and come to a determination about what the business is worth. I square that off against what the seller expects in terms of a selling price. And once we've agreed on those things and gathered all the necessary material, I put that into a confidential business profile. It's usually about 20 to 30 pages. That contains all of the information relative to the sale of the business and describes the business location, the financial statements, the tax returns, and the reconciliation of those two pieces of information. Then I calculate an owner benefit or a cash flow.

Meanwhile, we've listed the property or the business anonymously on about six or seven different worldwide websites specializing in buying and selling businesses. These have a vast audience worldwide. Prospective buyers go to these websites, click on the businesses they are interested in and are linked to the listing broker. If it's my listing, the inquiry will come directly to me. If they are dealing with another broker, I will cooperate with that broker. If the prospective buyer comes directly to me, which is 90% of the time, I go through a qualification process for that buyer. I need to know who I'm dealing with and obtain credentials regarding driver's license, address, etc. And most importantly, I need to know their experience and proof of funds. I need to know that they have the financial wherewithal to buy a business because businesses typically sell from $300,000 to $5 or $6 million in our space.

Once I have qualified the buyer, I can release the confidential business profile and have them sign a confidentiality agreement. I may also speak to the seller to get their approval to move forward. The buyer then receives all of the relevant information to the business. The final step is a meeting with the seller, onsite or offsite.

■ Is there anything else you would like to share?

René Brandon: My advice is to do the research. Find a broker you are compatible with. Don't just settle for the first broker you come across. Network, do your homework and do multiple Google searches. It would be best to speak to several brokers to get a sense of where they are coming from and whether or not they can help you reach your goals.

■ How can people find you, connect with you, and learn more?

René Brandon: My website is www.leopardbiz.com. When you go to the homepage, you will see my mugshot, several videos, and a menu. All of my information is on the contact page.

Florida Business Exchange, Inc. does not verify or warrant the veracity of any information provided from business sellers to business buyers, or vice-versa, nor does it guarantee the accuracy of any representations, data, calculations or valuations. As required by Florida law, Florida Business Exchange, Inc. is a Transaction Broker and, by definition, does not represent or maintain a fiduciary duty to either buyer or seller. You should not assume that Florida Business Exchange, Inc. has verified any information that it has acquired and provided to you. Buyers and Sellers are responsible to independently test, challenge and verify the accuracy, completeness, and veracity of all information provided to them directly or indirectly by any party. Nothing contained herein is intended to constitute legal, accounting, or tax advice. Florida Business Exchange, Inc. strongly encourages you to seek independent legal counsel from an attorney who is a member of the Florida bar and a certified public accountant who is licensed to practice in the state of Florida. Nothing herein is intended to constitute the sale of any security as defined in the Securities Act of 1933 or to constitute investment advice as defined in the Investment Company Act of 1940.

RENÉ BRANDON

M&A Advisor/Broker Associate

Leopard Business/Florida Business Exchange

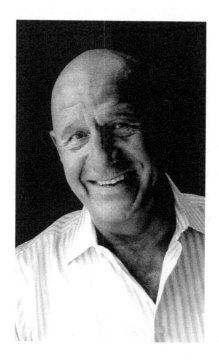

René Brandon provides executive management, consulting, advisory and mentoring, and financial services to business owners and entrepreneurs and is a professional M&A Advisor and Licensed Broker. Spanning 50+ years, René built an extensive business career with global and private companies. He has been hands-on as an owner, scaling start-ups and managing turnarounds and privately-owned companies. Sales $500,000 – $125,000,000. He managed five to twelve hundred teammates in the USA, Canada, and Australia. As a top salesman, he quickly moved up the corporate ladder, through various positions to CEO of several companies, and successfully moved across different industries, including "brick and mortar" – software technology.

René has a rare combination of business savvy and professional CEO management and financial experience in large, complex corporations and small to large entrepreneurial organizations. He has worked internationally with Fortune 500 and privately-owned companies.

René is a hands-on, results-oriented leader with a proactive management style. He has held senior executive positions as CEO, President, and VP/General Manager with Transfirst International, GE, Eaton Industrial, and Xerox. He has significant experience in mergers and acquisitions, joint ventures, and financial restructuring of productive assets. He has personally been involved in over 300 business transactions across a broad range of industries.

He is a strategic thinker responsible for several turnarounds; his people management skills, strengths in planning and execution, and financial management enable him to achieve results quickly and successfully. His enthusiastic, innovative, and decisive leadership spans several industries working with companies in the USA, Canada, Australia, and Europe.

Integrity is foremost for René; his passions are marketing and treating people with respect and dignity. To learn more, call or email for a free initial consultation.

EMAIL:
rb@leopardbiz.com

PHONE:
941-402-4844

WEBSITE:
www.leopardbiz.com

FACEBOOK:
https://www.facebook.com/LeopardBiz/

YOUTUBE:
https://www.youtube.com/channel/UCcPHjWcw-N6KrPoaaarZWgw

LINKEDIN:
https://www.linkedin.com/company/leopardbiz/

BUSINESS BROKERS OF FLORIDA:
https://bbfmls.com/

INTERNATIONAL BUSINESS BROKERS ASSOCIATION:
https://www.ibba.org/

RON
EDMONDS

CONVERSATION WITH RON EDMONDS

■ **Ron, you are the founder of Principium Capital, LLC. Tell us about your work and the people you help.**

Ron Edmonds: We have a vertically focused merger & acquisition firm. We work with lawn and landscape companies and other similar services across the country, including tree care, vegetation management, snow & ice management, irrigation, sweeping, and other facility services.

■ **Do owners know where to start when it comes to selling a business?**

Ron Edmonds: They don't know where to begin for the most part. There has been so much attention on this particular industry that some players in the larger categories ($20 million and up in revenue) are constantly hounded by private equity and other investors. Some of them have gotten a little bit savvier, but for the most part, their level of knowledge is low regarding the business selling process. That being said, our most successful client engagements have involved clients we have known and worked with for an extended period, sometimes over ten years. Clients find us by word-of-mouth referrals, our involvement with industry associations and publications, and a robust web presence.

■ What questions and concerns do business owners have when they reach out to you?

Ron Edmonds: They want to know the value of their business, which is a pretty difficult question to answer when it comes down to it. There isn't a rule of thumb. Most business owners think that because they heard "John down the road sold for seven times EBITDA," they can do the same thing. They don't realize that the guy down the street may not be telling the truth, the calculation might be different, and he might not even have records to support those numbers.

Business owners have many concerns about the sales process. Typically, their top concerns are ensuring that the process is handled confidentially and that they get the best deal possible.

■ As we are coming out of a pandemic, is it a good time to buy or sell a business? What have you seen in your market?

Ron Edmonds: The market has been unbelievable, and it's really hard to imagine that a pandemic year could be the best year ever. We've been in this business for 17 years. And there's no doubt that 2021 stands out as the best year ever. I believe 2022 will exceed 2021. The phenomenon of going into a pandemic is that in March and April of 2020, people like me thought the world was ending. We thought we would never be able to sell another business. But after two or three months, it became evident that was the farthest thing from the truth. It was actually triggering buyers. One of the things we found is that this particular industry was almost counter-cyclical to the economic downturns related to the pandemic. People spent more money on landscaping-related services, both commercial and residential. People realized the strength of this type of investment versus other industries that were much more heavily impacted. The strong market has been continuing in 2022 despite economic uncertainty.

■ How do you help owners sell their businesses?

Ron Edmonds: First, we sort out the facts and help the seller understand what is possible and how to position their business for sale. There's no doubt that owners who have been most successful in exit transactions have been the ones who had planned for years and years prior. One of the most successful deals I have worked on involved talking to the sellers for ten years. Now, that certainly isn't the norm because I am usually getting someone who says, "It's time for me to sell my business; let's get after it!" I have very little time to work through the things that will build value and improve the process on short notice. Ideally, we want time to work on improving the value of the business, creating an approach that allows them to maximize value through competitive offers and, therefore, getting the best deal possible.

When a client's business is ready to "go to market," we use a structured approach to move the process efficiently and work hard to achieve the best results for our clients. We prepare a selling document that effectively tells the client's story and prepare a buyer list to approach. We have an advantage with our deep industry knowledge and relationships. The actual sales process is tailored to the needs of each particular client. For larger clients, we often use a "two-step auction" that involves soliciting indications of interest from a large group of potential buyers, evaluating the indications of interest, and then soliciting offers from selected buyers who submitted indications of interest.

We walk with our clients through negotiating a letter of intent, due diligence, document preparation and negotiations, resolving issues that develop during the process, closing the transaction, and resolving any post-closing matters.

■ **Statistics show that 80% of businesses that go to market never sell. What are the reasons for this?**

Ron Edmonds: The biggest one is unrealistic expectations and thinking your business is worth more than it is, then being unwilling to accept a realistic offer. People compare their business to other businesses, which is never an accurate gauge of value. To get the highest price, it has to be a solid business with excellent growth potential and a substantial margin. The businesses that draw the highest valuations in the lawn and landscape industry usually have a significant recurring revenue component, so they have people under a contract who pay them monthly. That lowers the risk to a buyer and makes higher valuations possible.

Another common reason businesses don't sell is having the wrong advisor handle the sale. Some business brokers are not very proactive in getting deals done. They spend all their time getting listings knowing that a percentage of their listings will sell. Sometimes brokers do not have a good understanding of the industry their client operates in. You certainly don't have to use an industry specialist, but if you don't, your broker needs to invest the time and energy to understand the industry and its unique attributes.

■ Ron, what inspired you to get started in this field?

Ron Edmonds: I worked for a Big Four accounting firm for 14 years, followed by eight years in the industry. I then took some time to decide what I wanted to do with the rest of my career. In the meantime, I did some consulting work. I ended up consulting for the largest lawn care company in the country. They were going through a significant business transformation. They primarily obtained new customers through telemarketing. However, the "no-call list" severely restricted telemarketing. As one solution, they significantly ramped up their acquisition program and did many deals yearly. They wanted someone to give it a fresh look and help them develop an efficient process for moving potential deals through their pipeline and completing them. Initially, I thought it would be a 90-day project, and it ended up being most of my time for three or four years. I had the opportunity to interact with business brokers who sold the lawn care companies my client was buying. Frankly, I thought, "Wow, I can't imagine business owners really like working with these people. And there must be business owners who would rather deal with someone who was a little more analytical and less hard sell. Not to mention someone who actually understood their business." I saw a big opportunity there, got involved with some industry groups, and launched Principium. It was the perfect start to this new chapter for me.

By concentrating on mergers & acquisitions in a vertical market and actively writing, speaking, and developing relationships in that industry, I sort of became a big fish in a little pond, exactly the opposite of what I had been earlier in my career. Potential clients began to seek me out - and I have loved every minute of it.

■ Is there anything else you would like to share?

Ron Edmonds: If you want to sell your business, thinking about timing is a good idea. It is very difficult to time the sale of your business. While we're in an extraordinarily strong climate right now, the M&A world has always been cyclical, and you can't count on when you'll be able to sell your business. So if you're looking at your situation and know that you need to be out of the business or retire five years from now, you can't count on the ideal market when you need to exit. You would be well advised to explore the market and be ready to go when the time is right, rather than waiting until the last minute.

That being said, if you have the luxury of some time, there are often concrete steps you can take to improve the value of your business. In most cases, going through the process of identifying and implementing changes that can improve the value of your business is well worth it. Those same changes are likely to make your business stronger, more resilient, and more profitable, whether you ultimately sell the business or not. Some business owners who go through that process will discover that retaining their business and identifying a manager to run the business will produce a better financial outcome for them (and, potentially, their employees and customers) than a sale.

■ **How can people find you, connect with you, and learn more?**

Ron Edmonds: The best way is to visit our website at www.principiumgroup.com. Business owners will find tools and information helpful in understanding and navigating the selling process. They can also call us at 888-229-5740 or email info@principiumgroup.com.

RON EDMONDS

Founder

Principium Capital, LLC

Ron Edmonds is the managing member of Principium Capital, a leading advisory firm serving the lawn and landscape industry in the areas of mergers & acquisitions and exit planning. He also works with tree care, vegetation management, snow and ice management, and other facility services.

For sellers, he advises on preparing businesses for sale and represents sellers by marketing their businesses. For buyers, he assists in developing strategic plans for acquisitions, identifying targets, facilitating negotiations, structuring transactions, and conducting due diligence investigations. He is an advisor to private equity groups and others interested in the industry and also extensively consults on business valuation and exit planning.

Ron is an expert in green industry mergers and acquisitions, having played a key role in hundreds of transactions over the past twenty years. He is the author of *Green Exit – Exit Planning for Green Industry Business Owners,* along with two other books. He publishes an electronic newsletter, Green Industry M&A News. He regularly publishes reports on Private Equity Investment in the Landscape Industry and Valuation Trends in the Landscape Industry.

He is frequently quoted in industry publications and has had numerous articles published in industry publications, including *Landscape Management* and *Lawn & Landscape.* He is a frequent speaker at industry and corporate events.

He is a member of the National Association of Landscape Professionals, the Tree Care Industry Association, M&A Source, the Alliance of Merger & Acquisition Advisors, and the Association for Corporate Growth.

Ron holds BS and MS degrees in accounting from Oklahoma State University and previously worked with a Big Four accounting firm.

He is based in Memphis, Tennessee, but serves clients throughout the U.S. and, occasionally, internationally.

EMAIL:

redmonds@principiumgroup.com

PHONE:

888-229-5740

WEBSITE:

https://principiumgroup.com

SHERYL
VAZQUEZ

CONVERSATION WITH SHERYL VAZQUEZ

■ **Sheryl, you are the founder of CSG Capital. Tell us about your work and the people you help.**

Sheryl Vazquez: I am the founder and CEO of CSG Capital, powered by EXP Commercial. I am a commercial broker. I am also a member of IBBA, specializing in restaurants primarily, although I work with some retail spaces. My background is in restaurants, so I know what is needed for upfitting, what to look for when selling, and inventory elements.

■ **Do restaurant owners know where to begin when it comes to selling their businesses?**

Sheryl Vazquez: Many of them don't. It involves keeping track of ongoing inventory, accounts payable, and accounts receivable. All of that needs to be considered, and you might want to do that outside of the deal in a bill of sale. Since it is constantly moving, you can have inventory specialists come in the day before closing to handle things like liquor.

> ■ **The pandemic hit the restaurant industry hard. What is it like to sell a restaurant in today's market?**

Sheryl Vazquez: Many restaurant owners are considering selling, mainly because restaurants, like office spaces, are morphing into ghost kitchens, food trucks, and commissaries. Most restaurant owners are looking at concepts that are more accessible to the consumer. Some food trucks want to get into brick and mortar, while others want to leave that space, so the struggle lately has been finding workers to stay based on what and how they are being paid. So this is a struggle for restaurants in general. Since the pandemic, we've seen restaurants move toward community-type kitchens.

> ■ **Where did all of the restaurant staff go?**

Sheryl Vazquez: I think many people are still struggling to find their own thing. Coming out of the pandemic, many people want to become entrepreneurs. So that's what is happening. However, there are still people looking for day-to-day jobs. They jump in and out of restaurants, perhaps not satisfied with how certain ones operate.

The business owners need to regroup and figure out how to find and keep employees.

◼ What are some ways to survive in today's post-pandemic restaurant market?

Sheryl Vazquez: It's important to innovate different ways to stay open and draw people in. Restaurants really need to have a strong "to-go" center and a key niche. For example, I've seen many fry bars opening up, french fries with tons of stuff piled on top. Is it good for you? Probably not. But people love it. So it would be best if you found that niche. Another example would be "to-go" adult beverages, such as muddled cocktails, that are difficult for people to make at home. As an owner, if you can think outside of the box, it might be a way to create new business.

◼ Is it a good time to sell a restaurant?

Sheryl Vazquez: It is an excellent time to sell, mainly because so many entrepreneurs out there want to start their own businesses. If you are considering selling, you need to have your paperwork together. It needs to be easy for someone like me to come in and look at the financials and determine what your business can sell for. I consider the market, the city, and the location to match the right buyers with sellers.

∎ How do you help owners sell their businesses?

Sheryl Vazquez: I look at assets, accounts payable, and what they have on hand that will be included in the sale. When I have buyers looking for restaurants, I consider what is important to them so I can easily match a buyer and a seller. Many restaurant owners will not have all the necessary items detailed, and sometimes it gets messy. That's where I step in and evaluate where assets and liabilities go. What's the capital? What area should we put that in? Then I can give an accurate valuation of the business so the owner knows what it is worth.

∎ Do buyers understand the impact the pandemic had on restaurants?

Sheryl Vazquez: Most of them understand. We've all been through it. Everyone is aware of what's going on with the numbers, especially in 2021. It was very difficult for restaurants and hospitality to achieve the desired numbers. I found that many restaurants lately have been offering coupons or special nights to drive people in. Business has increased because people have cabin fever and want to return to their local spots. Regulars are coming back, and business has been good, just not as good as before the pandemic.

■ Sheryl, what inspired you to get started in this field?

Sheryl Vazquez: I was a bartender for 30 years. I started bartending in Boston, moved to North Carolina, and continued bartending in the business areas. So most of my clients worked for IBM and similar companies. Then I decided to get into real estate. And when I got into real estate, I wanted to get into commercial immediately. I'm all about the business deal. I thought it sounded perfect when I got into commercial, and EXP offered business brokerage. So I'm doing both; selling the real estate and the business. It seemed like a no-brainer to specialize in restaurants since I had worked in them for 30 years and know what it is like.

■ Is there anything else you would like to share?

Sheryl Vazquez: Not many people know this, but I am a Feng Shui consultant. So I walk into a space and feel the area's energy and how it flows. I can help restaurant owners make minor adjustments to make the space feel lighter or airier. Not only will customers want to come in and enjoy a great meal, but buyers will also find it more attractive. The music, the setting, the scent, and the general feeling of the restaurant all come into play. So I can help set sellers up for success that way as well.

■ **How can people find you, connect with you, and learn more?**

Sheryl Vazquez: My website is www.csgcapitals.com. You can also email me at sheri.vazquez@csgcapitals.com.

SHERYL VAZQUEZ, NCREA, CREIPS, GRI

Founder and CEO

CSG Capital, powered by EXP Commercial

Member of: IBBA, CVBBA, TCAR,
Durham Chamber of Commerce

Sheryl Vazquez is a commercial and business broker in the Raleigh-Durham area of North Carolina. She founded CSG Capital, LLC, powered by EXP Commercial, and is the operating CEO of the company. Her background in the restaurant industry runs back 30 years, which gives her an intimate knowledge of the industry and how to sell and purchase the business for owners. She is a certified Graduate Realtor Institute, National Commercial Real Estate Advisor, Certified Real Estate Investment Planner, certified mentor, new agent course creator, member of the International Business Broker Association, Carolina-Virginia Business Broker Association, Durham Chamber of Commerce, Triangle Commercial Association of Realtors, and has sat on the legislative committee with the Durham Association of Realtors.

EMAIL:

sheri.vazquez@csgcapitals.com

PHONE:

919-619-6863

WEBSITE:

https://www.csgcapitals.com

FACEBOOK:

https://www.facebook.com/expcommercial

INSTAGRAM:

https://www.instagram.com/sherylvazquezbroker/

LINKEDIN:

https://www.linkedin.com/in/sheryl-vazquez-bab04a147/

MICHAEL
SCHWANTES

MICHAEL SCHWANTES

CONVERSATION WITH MICHAEL SCHWANTES

■ **Michael, you are the owner of CBS-Global /
Creative Business Services. Tell us about
your work and the people you help.**

Michael Schwantes: We are based in Green Bay, Wisconsin, and Wisconsin is our primary market. We get outside the Wisconsin market from time to time since we have specialty areas in the M&A realm in addition to our Main Street practice. We are the number one M&A broker in the dairy industry. We sell a lot of cheese and dairy companies. Being from Wisconsin and knowing the marketplace, this is attractive to many of our sellers starting to age out. Many started these businesses when they were very young; I always say they had one hammer, and now they have ten. They are interested in retiring on a very confidential basis. They bring us in to prepare them for sale, package the business up, and take them to a strategic audience of buyers just for that industry.

■ Do owners know where to start when it comes to selling a business?

Michael Schwantes: They don't know where to begin. Like that old saying, "It's lonely at the top," they often don't know where to go for help. They think their attorney will charge them too much. Their best friend has their own problems with their business. So when it comes to exiting, they really need help. Even if it is two to four years before they are ready to sell, we come in to help them prepare. For the business to be appropriately packaged, we have to consider components like real estate appraisals, machinery and equipment appraisals, and the valuation of the business itself. Many segments need to come together simultaneously to make the business marketable. One thing we are always in tune with is the passion of the seller. Passion is everything. And if that seller has lost their passion before being taken to market, it can be disastrous as far as pricing. A smart buyer knows when a seller has lost their passion. The buyer will see if the seller is still excited about the business.

■ What is your role in helping owners sell their businesses?

Michael Schwantes: Most people we work with started or inherited their businesses, and now they want to do something else with their lives. Perhaps there was a death in the family or personal challenges causing them to need to exit. But waiting until an event forces you to sell is *not* a good time to plan your exit. The time to prepare your business for sale is when you are at the top of your game, the industry is doing well, and your employees are sound. It's essential to take the time to prepare key employees because a buyer is paying for goodwill and expecting those employees to continue providing excellent service. Right now, employment is a challenge for many companies. So the smart seller not only prepares their business for sale but prepares their employees for sale, making sure they are in the correct positions and being paid well. Then they will be less likely to exit when the new buyer takes over the business.

■ Is this a good time to sell a business? What have you seen in your market?

Michael Schwantes: We had a record year last year. I was going over numbers for this year, and it appears we will exceed last year because so many strategic buyers are looking to acquire. Private equity is big, with family offices out there looking as well. Our biggest challenge is finding strategic buyers and pricing the businesses fairly. We have many more buyers than sellers because there are still rollups going on. For example, we do a lot in the medical staffing industry nationwide. Many strategic buyers are rolling up medical staffing companies. Some markets, such as the convenience store market, are a little more challenging. We have a company called Kwik Trip with 800 stores in the Midwest, and it's more difficult to sell these stores than it would have been ten years ago. So every situation has some uniqueness to it. Even though there are more buyers than sellers, many owners are starting to age out and think about selling. And frankly, many business owners are making a lot of money right now, so they want to stick it out for a couple more years in those cases. But I would advise you not to stick it out too long. You might lose a window of opportunity with interest rates increasing and the economy slowing down.

■ Michael, what inspired you to get started in this field?

Michael Schwantes: I started the company in 1979, 43 years ago, but I owned many restaurants in my time. I was raised in Door County, which is very well known to many people in Chicago and Milwaukee. I had five restaurants by the time I was 27. I sold them myself, and one of my best friends started a company called Jellystone Campgrounds. One day he asked me, "What are you going to do?" I just got accepted to a law school in Michigan, and he said, "You don't want to be an attorney. You just sold all of your businesses yourself. Why don't you become a business broker?" There weren't many business brokers back then. I think I was one of maybe a few in Wisconsin. But in the Door County area, many businesses get transferred. So we were the top business broker in Door County for many years, and we still are, but we moved the office to Green Bay about 25 years ago. Now we have expert agents that specialize in many industries. I personally sell a lot of transportation companies and restaurants. It is very satisfying to bring two people together, helping one exit and the other create new opportunities for their family. It's a rewarding profession.

◼ Is there anything else you would like to share?

Michael Schwantes: I can only give guidance by saying, "Don't wait until the last minute." There are good business brokerage companies throughout the country. Do some research and interview more than one. Personality is important. Do you feel comfortable with the personality of the individual broker and the company itself? Every company has a unique personality. Make a decision, prepare your business for sale, but don't wait too long. When the passion goes away, the value starts to go away. Sell at the top of your game.

◼ How can people find you, connect with you, and learn more?

Michael Schwantes: We have offices in Green Bay, Wisconsin, and Oshkosh and Sheboygan. I can be reached at 920-432-1166. Ask for me; I would love to talk to you. I can also connect you with one of my qualified agents.

MICHAEL SCHWANTES

President & CEO, CBI, M&AMI

CBS-Global / Creative Business Services

In 1979, Michael founded CBS Global LLC as a business intermediary. By carefully considering all essential components involved in a successful transition, Michael is able to deliver consistently superior results to his clients around the world. These results are fueled partly by a customized marketing strategy utilizing state-of-the-art resources to represent buyers and sellers effectively.

His areas of expertise include real estate investments and 1031 Starker Exchanges. Michael's specific areas of specialization are mergers and acquisitions, manufacturing/distribution firms, and transportation companies.

Michael is a graduate of the University of Wisconsin-Stout. He has an extensive sales and consulting background, which aligns well with his ongoing postgraduate development. Additionally, he has earned M&AMI (Mergers and Acquisitions Master Intermediary) and CBI (Certified Business Intermediary) designations. His experience enables him to deliver expert advice in the business brokerage and mergers and acquisitions industry, with specific areas of expertise in the core manufacturing and distribution industries. Recently, Michael closed transactions in the medical, aviation, transportation, and food/dairy industries.

Michael continues to attend industry conferences. He is a member of the International Business Broker's Association (IBBA), M&A Source, Midwest Business Brokers and Intermediaries (MBBI), the National Association of Realtors (NAR), Wisconsin Realtors Association (WRA), Commercial Association of Realtors Wisconsin (CARW), New North, Wisconsin Cheese Makers Association (WCMA), Wisconsin Specialty Cheese Institute (WSCI), Wisconsin Motor Carriers Association (WMCA), Wisconsin Assisted Living Association (WALA), Wisconsin Restaurant Association (WRA), and the American Staffing Association (ASA).

Clients can trust Michael to consider all essential components of a successful transition carefully. He is tremendously dedicated to his clients and driven to deliver superior results consistently.

EMAIL:

mschwantes@cbs-global.com

PHONE:

920-432-1166

WEBSITE:

www.CBS-Global.com

OTHER:

https://cbs-global.com/our-team/michael-j-schwantes/

LINKEDIN:

https://www.linkedin.com/in/mikeschwantes/

NICHOLAS BROWN

CONVERSATION WITH NICHOLAS BROWN

> ■ **Nicholas, you are the Head of Mergers and Acquisitions with Dragonflip. Tell us about your work and the people you help.**

Nicholas Brown: Dragonflip was founded in 2017 in Germany, which is where our co-founders are from. We specialize in the mergers and acquisitions of eCommerce businesses. We're usually working with a single owner or a small group of business owners who started growing their eCommerce businesses on Amazon or Shopify, expanded, and are looking to exit because maybe they don't have the internal resources to continue growing and have their brands reach potential. So they come to us, and we help prepare their businesses, prepare them for market and provide a valuation. We help our clients navigate every step of the sales process - from the initial valuation until the money is in their hands post due diligence.

■ **As we are coming out of a pandemic, is it a good time to sell an eCommerce business? What have you seen in your market?**

Nicholas Brown: I've been in this industry since 2015. So I was there when the normal valuations and exit multiples were around 2.5x. Since the pandemic, there has been a large influx of "Amazon aggregators," investment groups coming in with a lot of money to buy quality Amazon brands. They use economies of scale to aggregate a number of brands under one umbrella and grow and expand to other marketplaces outside Amazon or the United States like Europe, Australia, and even Asia.

The pandemic increased eCommerce sales significantly over the past two years, and the average exit multiple grew as a result. The average multiple has gone from 2.5x to 4x. I've seen some exits as high as 5x and 6x because there's so much capital in the market looking for quality brands. So I would say it's been a pretty good time to sell your business, especially in 2020 and 2021. Going into 2022, we've noticed a little bit of evening out or normalization of these multiples. In addition to inflation, the war in Ukraine has had an impact, especially on the buyers and sellers living in Europe. It's still a pretty advantageous buyer's market, but we haven't seen the steady increase of exit multiples in 2022 that we saw in 2020 and 2021.

■ **Have these multiples sparked an interest in selling that wasn't there before?**

Nicholas Brown: We have seen interest increase with higher multiples and awareness of the term "Amazon aggregator." At Dragonflip, we have had a significant increase in valuation requests. Once we use our experience and internal modeling to provide a valuation, business owners are more interested in exiting if they see 4x+ multiples. Owners are contemplating, "Should I continue to work four more years, or should I exit now, start something else, and exit that business in four years?" So we've definitely seen an influx of interest from business owners deciding that now is the time to exit.

■ **Do eCommerce business owners know where to begin when it comes to selling?**

Nicholas Brown: It's a mix. I've worked with Amazon and eCommerce business owners who have exited a previous brand and go into the process with the knowledge they need to build a quality brand. For example, they are aware that a brand will have a higher valuation multiple if the products offered by the brand are all related, as opposed to a random collection of products.

We also work with business owners that started a side hustle on Amazon, Etsy, or Shopify, left their original jobs, and are now 100% focused on fulfillment and growing the brand. Because the business was not their primary focus when they started, they put very little thought into exiting. A couple of brokerage firms in the United States and Europe specialize in digital asset sales, but far fewer specialize in eCommerce like Dragonflip. There just isn't as much specialization as you would see in brick-and-mortar brokerage firms. We started Dragonflip to let business owners know that if they are looking to sell their eCommerce business, we are a more specialized brokerage firm and can help them do it successfully.

■ What are the most important things to make an eCommerce business attractive for sale?

Nicholas Brown: I will give you the top three. The first thing is high-quality financials. The first recommendation I make to every business owner we work with is to hire a CPA or an accountant to help get their finances in shape to go to market. Nothing deteriorates trust faster between a buyer and a seller than questionable financials. You want to prove to the market that you have run your business well and have the financials to back it up.

Financial trends are another key issue. The buyer market will pay a premium for businesses that are growing year over year and meet a certain level of profitability. At Dragonflip, we have found that if an eCommerce business has 30% revenue growth year over year and net profit margins of over 25%, the exit multiple will increase significantly.

Lastly, we look at the quality of the brand. You want a cohesive product offering with business products that complement each other rather than a random array of products under your brand name. It is also essential to have some protection in terms of IP, patents, trademarks, or even having many positive reviews about your product. If a buyer is looking at two products on Amazon, one with 2,000 reviews and the other with 200, they are going with the product with the higher number of reviews because there is more evidence of a quality product. If you have these things to protect your brand and prove its quality, it will increase your valuation multiple.

■ Nicholas, what inspired you to get started in this field?

Nicholas Brown: I started at Flippa, a marketplace like eBay, but for digital assets. It was my first job after finishing my MBA, and I had no experience in the industry. I found that I loved speaking with business owners about why they initially started their businesses and helping them exit to reap all the benefits of the work they put into creating the business. I was drawn to working with entrepreneurs and learning about the various valuation drivers for different niches - SaaS, eCommerce, or Content. I did not plan to enter this industry when I was in college, but after I learned about Flippa and M&A for digital assets, it was all very enticing to me, so I stayed in that lane.

■ Is there anything else you would like to share?

Nicholas Brown: The most important thing for any business owner to know is the current valuation of their business. At Dragonflip, we offer free valuation services because we believe it is so important. Knowing the true market value of your business will help you assess business opportunities, and it will help you form your exit plan. It gives you so much information and another way to monitor year-over-year growth if you know how your valuation has changed each year.

■ How can people find you, connect with you, and learn more?

Nicholas Brown: My website is www.dragonflip.com. We have a valuation calculator, and a link will allow you to set up a meeting with me. I'm happy to speak with business owners about their valuation and the sales process. You can email me at nicholas@dragonflip.com.

NICHOLAS BROWN, MBA, MPA, CBI

Head of Mergers and Acquisitions

Dragonflip

Nicholas is the Head of M&A at Dragonflip. He has worked in mergers and acquisitions since 2015 and holds the Certified Business Intermediary designation from the IBBA. Nicholas has a Master's in Business Administration from the University of Florida and a Master's in Public Administration from the University of Southern

California. He enjoys distilling complex business concepts into effective sales materials and working closely with his clients to source quality investment opportunities and facilitate fair, equitable deals. Nicholas has successfully brokered dozens of deals and developed an extensive network of SaaS and eCommerce investors.

Before Nicholas' career in M&A, he worked in the corporate finance and legal sectors, gaining experience in business analysis, contract negotiation, and strategic planning. He is adept at utilizing data from diverse financial and information systems to build tools and make recommendations that improve organizational decision-making and increase profitability.

Nicholas grew up in Baton Rouge, Louisiana, and currently resides in Stockholm, Sweden.

EMAIL:
Nicholas@dragonflip.com

PHONE:
1 (650) 488-4532

WEBSITE:
www.dragonflip.com

CONVERSATION WITH PHIL WOLFSTEIN

■ **Phil, you are a business broker with ZOOM Business Brokers. Tell us about your work and the people you help.**

Phil Wolfstein: I'm a Certified Business Broker with ZOOM Business Brokers in California. There are hundreds of business brokers in California; however, there were only 57 Certified Business Brokers at last count. I help business owners find qualified buyers for their businesses. A lot goes into the process, including forming an exit strategy, taking the business to market, working with buyers, vetting the buyers, going through due diligence, conditions release, working with landlords, and taking the business through a successful close of escrow. People think selling a business is an event, but it's not. It's a process. It's an emotional and life-changing experience, equivalent to graduating college, getting married, buying a house, or having children.

I work with businesses that are half a million in sales to $15 million with three to 50 employees. I frequently work as part of a team with commercial realtors, financial advisors, business advisors, CPAs, and transactional attorneys. All of these people are involved in getting a business owner ready to sell.

■ How informed are business owners when it comes to selling a business?

Phil Wolfstein: Business owners and entrepreneurs as a group are go-getters. They are typically very good at growing the business and increasing sales, as those are the things they do best. But most business owners don't even think about transitioning or selling their business. I heard that 80% or more business owners have never even looked at succession planning. They just assume that it will take care of itself, or perhaps they will transfer ownership within the family. But that mindset needs to change. The baby boom generation of business owners must ask themselves, "What do I need to do?" And it always begins with a broker opinion of value to determine what their business is worth and if there are buyers for the business.

◼ Are there myths and misconceptions about selling a business?

Phil Wolfstein: Having been a small business owner for over 25 years in the import/export trading business, I know that business owners don't have time to focus on the day they exit the business. They are just focused on running the business. The biggest challenge for business brokers is making people aware that there are professionals who can help them market and sell their business. Business owners often have questions like, "How am I going to sell my business?" and "What's my business worth?" A business broker can help answer those questions. I can help highlight what aspects of the business need to be focused on to get the highest value. We also discuss the motivation for selling to prepare the business in the best way possible to go to market and get the best price.

◼ Statistics show that 80% of businesses that go to market never sell. What are the reasons for this?

Phil Wolfstein: I'm a little different from most business brokers because between 70% and 80% of the businesses I list actually close escrow. The average is about 20% to 25%. Four out of five businesses that list don't actually sell and close escrow. The two biggest reasons are books and records and landlord-related issues. Books and records need to be clean and accurate to give the buyer a clear picture of what is going on with your business. You don't want surprises popping up after signing a letter of intent or purchase agreement. Everybody in the segment I work in has excellent relationships with their landlords; they love me and are all great guys. But when it comes down to negotiating a lease assumption or a new long-term lease for a qualified buyer, that can become a significant barrier to getting the deal done.

Today, there is an added barrier to selling a business, directly resulting from the "Great Resignation." Finding talented employees, compensating them, and keeping them has been a key issue for buyers. Once the business is acquired, the buyer wants to be assured that key employees will stay on to ensure continuity of cash flow, business operations, and future growth. So the employees have become an increasingly important aspect in the sales of businesses I work with.

■ **As we are coming out of a pandemic, is it a good time to sell a business? What have you seen in your market?**

Phil Wolfstein: I think it's a great time to sell. It's the perfect storm. Even though the baby boom generation is moving to retirement faster than anticipated, there is still a shortage of good, profitable businesses relative to the demand. So it is definitely a seller's market. Multiples are steady to slightly higher in particular markets such as manufacturing. Due to higher interest rates, COVID, the "Great Resignation," labor issues, and supply chain issues, we expect to see many more well-run businesses coming to market in 2022 and

2023. It may shift to a buyer's market in 2023 or 2024, but right now, there is a strong buyer interest in all segments. Financing is still very attractive, and SBA and 504 loans are available. More and more millennials are looking to buy jobs and transition from large corporate America to running their own business. These components make it a great time to go to market now, rather than waiting another two or three years.

■ Phil, what inspired you to get started in this field?

Phil Wolfstein: That's a funny question. I was in the trading business for many years and had my own company. In 2001 and 2002, I transitioned into business consulting and development, mainly because I was doing red meat exports and Mad Cow Disease was a hard barrier to overcome. I have always had a passion for real estate and have enjoyed buying and selling real estate in my personal life. I decided to get my license about eight or nine years ago. I found that selling residential and commercial real estate wasn't a great fit for me because I felt like I wasn't the 20-something with a Ferrari or a 25-year veteran with a book of business and referrals.

Then I got introduced to business brokering. It's a unique business and one of the few areas where your experience and expertise really work for you. There's no glass ceiling. If you're looking to sell and market your business, you want somebody with some depth, experience, knowledge, and compassion. You need someone to give you that 10,000-foot view of how to get from here to there and handle the emotional aspect of selling a business. It's an emotional decision and a significant financial decision. I am very passionate about helping business owners, their families, employees, vendors, and customers get through that process successfully. Once I got into business brokering and saw what I could bring to the table, I never looked back.

■ Is there anything else you would like to share?

Phil Wolfstein: If you are a business owner, you must start thinking about your exit strategy *now*. Even if the sale will be five years out and you are not sure if you will be selling to a family member, a neighbor, or a partner, you need to start planning now. Don't just assume that somebody will be waiting to snatch up your business when you are ready to sell. It's a much better approach to start now. If you aren't prepared, your books are a mess, and you don't know the value of your business, you can contact a business broker and start the conversation. It's like going to the doctor and having a physical to find your baseline. Finding out what your business is worth will almost always highlight what areas you need to focus on. I'm happy to help people start the process so they are ready for the day they decide to sell.

■ How can people find you, connect with you, and learn more?

Phil Wolfstein: You can find me on LinkedIn. My phone number is 310-663-2180. You can also email me at phil.wolfstein@zbbcorp. com. I offer a no-charge, introductory call to see what assistance or information I can provide if you want to know the value of your business or are thinking about selling your business.

PHIL WOLFSTEIN, CBB

Business Broker

ZOOM Business Brokers

Phil is a great listener and problem solver. He is focused on using his 30+ years of broad-based, hands-on experience and expertise to get you the best possible deal, whether buying or selling your business.

He is passionate about problem-solving and getting the deal right. The devil is in the details!

He is a member of the California Association of Business Brokers and the International Business Brokers Association. Phil will work with you to establish the true earnings of your business and then, using a comprehensive approach incorporating four different methodologies, determine a business valuation and provide an exit strategy for business owners. Once a valuation is agreed upon, he will market your business in the quickest, most effective way for the highest value on the market.

Phil seeks to build and maintain long-term, mutually beneficial business relationships with the clients he serves. He will work with you to address issues and answer any questions you may have regarding the process of buying or selling a business. His unique multicultural perspective helps to smooth out the bumps in the road, overcome the challenges inherent in buying or selling a business, and facilitate the successful conclusion of your transaction.

> "On the Plains of Hesitation bleach the bones of countless millions, who, at the Dawn of Victory, sat down to wait, and waiting – died!"
>
> — George W. Cecil

EMAIL:

phil.wolfstein@zbbcorp.com

PHONE:

310-663-2180

WEBSITE:

www.zoombusinessbrokers.com

LINKEDIN:

https://www.linked.com/in/pwolfstein/

BLOG:

https://zoombusinessbrokers.com/blog/team/phil-wolfstein/

BUSINESS INNOVATORS SPOTLIGHT:

https://businessinnovatorsmagazine.com/
spotlight-phil-wolfstein-of-zoom-business-brokers/

SHEILA SPANGLER

CONVERSATION WITH SHEILA SPANGLER

■ **Sheila, you are a business broker with Murphy Business Sales. Tell us about your work and the people you help.**

Sheila Spangler: I am a business broker, also known as a business intermediary. I help sellers take their businesses to market, find a buyer, and exit. I like to joke that I "help people get into and out of business." I love what I do, and I've been at it for about twelve years in two different stints. My last stint has been with Murphy Business Sales for six years. I am also a business appraiser. So I have a couple of certifications that allow me to do valuation work for clients who want to sell and for SBA lenders who hire me to prepare valuations for lending purposes.

■ Do owners know where to start when it comes to selling a business?

Sheila Spangler: No, many of them don't. BizBuySell is a website that does a survey every quarter. They survey business brokers and owners. Most of the time, owners haven't thought about their exit. Generally, by the time they call me, they have suffered one of the ten "Deadly Ds:" death, divorce, disease, dissension among owners, disaster, debt, disability, declining sales, disinterest, and distraction. One of these things may now be forcing them to exit, but actual exit planning hasn't typically occurred. There are folks out there who do exit planning. A book was written 15 years ago called "The $10 Trillion Opportunity" that predicted a tsunami of baby boomers exiting. I think it has been a slow trickle because baby boomers have been determined to hang on. But I see a lot more now than I did before, mainly because baby boomers are older. In some respects, the pandemic made them realize they will have an end to their life at some point, and perhaps now is the time to get out and sell or transition to the next generation.

■ As we are coming out of a pandemic, is this a good time to sell a business? What have you seen in your market?

Sheila Spangler: Interestingly enough, I've seen a lot of businesses do well during the pandemic. As I mentioned previously, I do a lot of valuation work. Though there might have been a dip in 2020, it came roaring back in 2021, and things are continuing to be on an upward trend in 2022. So yes, it was scary in March of 2020 when everyone was told to panic, and we all did. And, of course, the government gave out money for businesses to survive. But in many cases, business owners knuckled down, rode it out, and now they've done well in the past year and one-half.

> ■ **Statistics show that up to 80% of businesses that go to market never sell. What are some reasons for this?**

Sheila Spangler: One of the biggest reasons is that business owners don't get the advice and assistance they need. For example, when BizBuySell (www.bizbuysell.com) does its regular survey, the results show that businesses that don't sell haven't had any advice and counsel about how to sell a business. Keep in mind that anyone can list a business on BizBuySell —owner, business broker, or anyone! But those that generally don't sell haven't priced it correctly. Was a valuation performed to ensure the price made sense? Was a package put together so the buyer could understand your financials and see the potential of your business?

Think of it this way; if you, as a seller, show up with a dog-eared box of jumbled financials and tell a buyer you want a million dollars for your business, a buyer will not be able to figure it all out on their own. In many cases, Main Street business buyers have never purchased a business before and don't know how or where to start analyzing the information. Hiring an intermediary assists the owner by professionally packaging the financial details to determine a realistic asking price and determine if this is a financeable transaction with a lender. Does the buyer have the necessary amount down to qualify for financing? Is there adequate business cash flow to cover the proposed acquisition debt after paying a new owner a reasonable wage? Do the asking price and cash flow make sense? That's what gets the deal done. When you fail to put the financials in order, determine a reasonable asking price, and present the details professionally that make financial sense, selling your business becomes a crapshoot. The sale falls through because the potential buyer cannot understand the opportunity.

■ Are there myths and misconceptions about selling a business?

Sheila Spangler: A lot of the pushback is sometimes over the fee. Owners think, "Why would I pay a business broker to sell my business? I can do it myself." There are books written about how to sell your own business, but you have to be able to devote a significant amount of time to all of the things I have talked about. If somebody was motivated enough, maybe they could do it. But when you've never done it before, you will have to take your eyes off your business. Your business will suffer while you are trying to be a business broker. Business owners are smart, and they are risk-takers. They wouldn't have gone into business if they didn't believe in themselves. So they tend to think they can do anything.

There is an excellent book by John Warrillow called "The Art of Selling Your Business," and I recommend it to all of my clients. John created a webinar a couple of years ago where he identified three types of business owners: mountain climbers, freedom fighters, and technicians (John calls them craftspeople).

The mountain climbers are the people who have a vision, they go to Silicon Valley, and they raise a lot of money. They don't care what the business is, as long as they can grow it and make money when they sell.

The freedom fighters are the people who I do business with. They are entrepreneurs who have owned their businesses for 20 to 30 years, and the employees, customers, and vendors are like family. So when they are ready to sell, it is a very tough, emotional thing to let go of. I understand their connection to the business and help them get through the process. So it's a very different mindset from the mountain climbers.

The third group is generally sole proprietors, who really don't have a sellable business and work independently and tend to be skilled technicians. But freedom fighters, who make up about 24% (according to John Warrilow) of the market, are the people we work with.

■ **Sheila, what inspired you to get started in this field?**

Sheila Spangler: Well, it was kind of an accidental thing. I was a commercial lender for over 20 years. And then, one day, I thought, "I'm tired of working in corporate America. I'm tired of following the rules that I don't think make sense." So I wrote my own business plan and launched my practice. What I thought I would do and ended up doing changed, like many business owners when they started. I thought I would help people arrange financing for all different business acquisitions and real estate purchases. As it turned out, one of my first clients was a gentleman whose wife called me and said, "Hey, my husband wants to buy this business. It's listed over here with a business brokerage, but he wants someone to represent him and help him figure out if this is a good deal and how to get it financed."

At this point, as crazy as it sounds, I didn't even know what a business broker was. So I started down that path and then learned about the IBBA, the International Business Brokers Association. My friend had just gone through the training to become a Certified Business Intermediary, and he said, "Sheila, you don't know what you don't know. You need to get educated if you're going to do this." And he was right. So I signed up, and I got certified in 2006. There were a lot of things I didn't know. But the IBBA is a great support and educational opportunity for business brokers, and I highly recommend it. Attending the IBBA conferences, you meet brokers from all over the country and share thoughts and ideas. It's an excellent resource. So that's how I got started, and I love what I do.

> ■ **Is there anything else you would like to share with owners considering selling their businesses?**

Sheila Spangler: The thing to remember is that it is not an easy task to sell a business. It's an emotional process, though you may not realize it. For example, a few years ago, I had a client who was a banker with me, and then he hired me to help him buy a go-kart business. He said, "Sheila, this will only be about the numbers, right? The numbers have to work." And I said, "Well, I understand that. But what is your motivation for buying this business? Don't you want to have some fun with your son?" He said, "Well, yeah." So there was some emotion driving him. We would justify it with the numbers, but he wanted a go-kart business because it looked like fun.

When buying or selling a business, the numbers have to make sense because you don't want to do something totally irrational. But there is a reason people buy. Perhaps they can see themselves doing a better job growing that particular business. Owners sell because they are ready to retire or have another venture they want to pursue. However, one of the biggest concerns of any business owner is that they want to see their business carry on. They want their employees and customers to be taken care of, and they want the solid reputation of the business to live on. So I try to coach the buyers to be sensitive to the owners' position about the business. Even though a potential buyer may disagree with how the owners ran the business, remember the owners have gotten it this far, and perhaps the buyer can take it farther.

■ **How can people find you, connect with you, and learn more?**

Sheila Spangler: My websites are www.murphybusinessboise.com or www.sheilaspangler.com. I only focus on selling in Idaho. But if you live in another state, you can contact me, and I can set you up with someone who can help you.

SHEILA SPANGLER, CVA, BCA, CMAP, CBI

Business Broker

Murphy Business Sales

Sheila Spangler is a Boise, Idaho-based Certified Mergers & Acquisitions Professional and Business Appraiser with Murphy Business Sales. She specializes in business valuation and sales, negotiation, deal structure, and financing. She began her career in finance as Vice President of commercial lending with national and regional banks before transitioning to business brokerage and valuation.

Prior to joining Murphy Business, she led her own business brokerage firm for several years. She also launched a Business Resource Center for a regional bank and the Small Business (SBA) backed Women's Business Center program in Idaho, two business-consulting organizations focused on financial counseling and training for entrepreneurs. Sheila received the Certified Valuation Analyst (CVA) designation from the National Association of Certified Valuators and Analysts and the Business Certified Appraiser (BCA) credential from the International Society of Business Appraisers. She earned the Certified Mergers & Acquisitions Professional (CMAP) designation from Kennesaw State University and the Certified Business Intermediary (CBI) credential from the International Business Brokers Association.

Sheila received a master's level degree from Pacific Coast Banking School at the University of Washington and holds a B.A. degree, business emphasis, communication minor, from Boise State University. She is an Idaho real estate broker.

EMAIL:

s.spangler@murphybusiness.com

PHONE:

208-343-7007 (direct)

WEBSITE:

www.murphybusinessboise.com

OTHER:

https://www.sheilaspangler.com

LINKEDIN:

https://www.linkedin.com/in/sheilaspangler/

PHIL
HANEY

CONVERSATION WITH PHIL HANEY

■ **Phil, you are a business broker with Sunbelt Business Brokers and Advisors. Tell us about your work and the people you help.**

Phil Haney: Sunbelt is the place to buy and sell businesses and get business valuations. We're actually the largest business brokerage in the country. We're all independent. But there are about 275 independent organizations. I represent sellers and buyers, do all pre-due diligence and due diligence work, and get them into escrow. I also handle commercial and leases and small, medium, and large business mergers and acquisitions. We work in many industries, including restaurants, automotive, franchises, beauty salons, distribution centers, educational colleges, and custom manufacturing companies across the country and internationally in many cases.

I have over 40 years of senior executive management and experience operating large manufacturing companies in the United States. I have been a business broker for 21 years and owned Sunbelt Business

Brokers in Santa Clarita for many years. I joined my partner, who owns Sunbelt in Bakersfield, as a Senior Executive, and I also operate out of the Sunbelt Bakersfield location. I have a consulting company and do a lot of business, primarily in California and throughout the nation. I enjoy helping business owners sell their businesses, get certified valuations, get their financials in order, address employee and labor issues, and perform sales and marketing action plans and development tasks.

We have over 41 websites to access buyers and continually send out correspondence and monthly newsletters. We also get a large number of buyers from referrals. I belong to the Chambers of Commerce in Santa Clarita and Beverly Hills and have done much networking over the years. We probably have 30,000+ buyers in our system at any given time. I also belong to the California Association of Business Brokers, so I network with all of the brokers in California and real estate brokers who come to me for help because they typically don't understand the business side of things. We help many international clients who have purchased a home and are now looking to acquire a business. We work with several banks to get SBA loans to help our clients fund their purchases.

A little background on me; at a young 75 years old, I was a Captain in the military and on the DMZ in Korea and then in Vietnam. I also ran large divisions in the corporate world before my last 21 years as a business broker. I love buying and selling businesses and helping owners improve their business's value, create an exit strategy, or do other mergers and acquisitions. Perhaps they want to grow their business, or maybe they want to sell their business to pursue other passions. I can help them with all of that.

This is an excellent time for buyers to consider buying a business and having another income stream. Whether they're management executives or blue-collar workers, many buyers have been in the corporate world a long time, and they want to try something different. They want to achieve ownership and independence and grow a business to support their families.

■ Do owners know where to start when it comes to selling a business?

Phil Haney: Most sellers don't know where to begin. They come to us for direction, guidance, and valuations. A business is a bulk sale, which is much different from real estate. It's much more complicated because we have to look at their seller discretionary earnings, sales, inventory costs, employees, commercial property leases, furniture, fixtures, and equipment. Commercial purchases are separate from business purchases, so those cases involve two different sales. We have a ten-point structure for selling businesses that we review with our clients. We discuss pre-due diligence, representation agreements, commission structure, sales, marketing, and advertising campaigns.

With buyers, we spend a lot of time ensuring everyone signs an NDA, buyer profile, agency disclosure, and proof of funds. We can also help with SBA loans or getting equity out of their home to fund the purchase of the business. All communication takes place via private meetings, primarily on Zoom these days. We meet with the buyer and the seller so that the potential buyer understands the organization of the business and can obtain more details from the owner. We always follow up, look for an offer, and work through negotiations with the seller. Then we enter the due diligence phase, release of contingency, and go into escrow. The key is to have a win-win for the buyer and the seller.

■ Phil, what inspired you to get started in this field?

Phil Haney: I've always had an entrepreneurial spirit. I grew up in New York and have lived in California since 1982. My dad was an entrepreneur, so I grew up with the desire to become one myself. After the military, I worked in organizations such as Johnson and Johnson, Becton Dickinson Medical, and Smead Manufacturing and ran the West Coast for several corporations. I also worked in technology, electronics, and other consumer product corporations.

I've always been passionate about being a business owner and using my sales, marketing, and financial skills to be a caregiver. In other words, I am passionate about helping people get into business. And that's why I love what I do. I always have a passion for ensuring that the seller is successful and the buyer is successful in whatever they do. We follow everything through before we go into escrow, and the key is to treat everybody with dignity and respect. I love business. At 75 years young, I still love business and helping business owners.

That's why I have my consulting company as well. Doctors, lawyers, you name it, come to me for business advice.

■ How can people find you, connect with you, and learn more?

Phil Haney: My email is phil.haney@sunbeltnetwork.com. My website is https://www.bakersfield@sunbeltnetwork.com for the Bakersfield office. I also have another office in Santa Clarita. My cell phone number is 661-644-5313, and my office number is 661-476-5002. If you still prefer to use fax machines, my fax number is 661-476-5003.

I always look forward to helping buyers and sellers through a professional process that includes listening and compassion. Everything is completely confidential if you are a seller who would like to begin discussing the process. I can also help buyers determine their career paths and interests to ensure we find an excellent fit. The corporate world isn't the same as it once was, so we have several buyers always wanting to explore other options.

PHIL HANEY

Business Broker

Sunbelt Business Brokers and Advisors

Phil Haney is a highly motivated and passionate professional, an expert and specialist in business brokering for sellers and buyers and business valuation services, and also works on commercial, leasing, and real estate services. He has over 40 years of experience in senior-level positions such as president, COO, general management, consulting, facilitation, and coaching for large corporations and manufacturing divisions, along with entrepreneurial ventures with startups, turnarounds, and high-growth businesses. This includes all types of manufacturing companies, distribution, professional entities, retail, service-oriented, educational, technology, non-profit, and franchises. Phil is a graduate of Colorado State University, attended graduate school, and was a prior Captain in the United States Army.

EMAIL:

phil.haney@sunbeltnetwork.com

PHONE:

661-644-5313

WEBSITE:

Bakersfield@SunbeltNetwork.com

ABOUT THE PUBLISHER

Mark Imperial is a Best-Selling Author, Syndicated Business Columnist, Syndicated Radio Host, and internationally recognized Stage, Screen, and Radio Host of numerous business shows spotlighting leading experts, entrepreneurs, and business celebrities.

His passion is to discover noteworthy business owners, professionals, experts, and leaders who do great work and share their stories and secrets to their success with the world on his syndicated radio program titled "Remarkable Radio."

Mark is also the media marketing strategist and voice for some of the world's most famous brands. You can hear his voice over the airwaves weekly on Chicago radio and worldwide on iHeart Radio.

Mark is a Karate black belt; teaches Muay Thai and Kickboxing; loves Thai food, House Music, and his favorite TV shows are infomercials.

Learn more:

www.MarkImperial.com

www.BooksGrowBusiness.com

Made in the USA
Middletown, DE
14 September 2022

10440239R00084